C000008140

Changi

Singapore International Airport

Changi

Singapore International Airport

John K. Morton

Airlife
England

Copyright © 2001 John K. Morton

First published in the UK in 2001
by Airlife Publishing Ltd

British Library Cataloguing-in-Publication Data
A catalogue record for this book
is available from the British Library

ISBN 1 84037 215 X

All rights reserved. No part of this book may
be reproduced or transmitted in any form or by any
means, electronic or mechanical including
photocopying, recording or by any information
storage and retrieval system, without permission from
the Publisher in writing.

Typeset by Rowland Phototypesetting Ltd,
Bury St Edmunds, Suffolk.
Printed in Singapore by Kyodo Printing Co. (S'pore)
Pte Ltd.

Airlife Publishing Ltd
101 Longden Road, Shrewsbury, SY3 9EB, England
E-mail: airlife@airlifebooks.com
Website: www.airlifebooks.com

Acknowledgements

Without doubt, my thanks must first of all go to the CAAS (Civil Aviation Authority of Singapore), without whose help this book could not have been produced. In particular, I very much appreciate the initial preparatory work and subsequent time given to me by Angela Goh who accompanied me whilst in and around the airport, driving me to suitable positions for photography and regularly supplying me with ice-cold water to keep me cool during periods of high temperatures. To Angela and the rest of the corporate services (Public Relations) team, I wish to extend my heartfelt thanks.

Thanks are also due to the various airlines which approved my request for permission to photograph their aircraft for use in this title. In particular, I would like to place on record the assistance provided by Thai Airways and Singapore Airlines.

Finally, I thank my ever-supporting wife Margaret, who regularly accompanies me on my trips around the world giving her help and assistance whenever necessary. I also acknowledge her help in the preparation of this title during the proof-reading process.

Introduction

Singapore Changi Airport (IATA code SIN) commenced operations from Terminal One in July 1981. The airport is located on the eastern edge of Singapore and has an elevation of 7 metres above sea level. Two parallel runways (02L, 02R and 20L and 20R), each 60 metres wide and 4000 metres in length, are separated by a 1.64-kilometre gap which houses the terminal buildings. Terminal One's peak handling capacity is 4300 passengers per hour, and 16 million passengers per year currently use the 126 check-in counters therein. Travellers are well catered for and an area of more than 5000 square metres is devoted to shopping, where stores offer duty-free liquor, cigarettes and tobacco, cosmetics, electronic equipment, jewellery and Singapore souvenirs. More than 6000 square metres is devoted to food with 15 restaurants serving cuisine ranging from fast food to haute cuisine. More than 40 airlines operate from Terminal One.

Terminal Two commenced operations in November 1990 and operates independently of Terminal One. A fully automatic Skytrain provides transportation for passengers between the two terminals. Terminal Two's capacity is larger than that of Terminal One, and it has the capability to handle 4500 passengers per hour, currently 20 million per year. The shopping and restaurant areas in Terminal Two are much larger than those in Terminal One but also provide a similar service.

Changi Airfreight Centre is an area of 47 hectares containing seven cargo terminals with a cargo-handling capacity of 1.7 million tonnes. Cargo in all shapes and sizes comes and goes at all hours of the day and night, handled by the latest stacker and mechanised handling systems.

Changi has achieved a consistent record of accolades due to the foresight of the development of civil aviation in Singapore, the award most often being won is 'Best Airport in the World'. Construction at Changi is still not finished as in December 1996 a decision was made to go ahead with the construction of Terminal Three, designed to handle an additional 20 million passengers a year, bringing the total number of passengers to over 60 million a year. The Mass Rapid Transit (MRT) line is in the process of being extended and will serve the airport in 2001. Perhaps one day all airports will be like Singapore Changi, providing travellers with an efficient and comfortable start and finish to their journey.

All photographs in this title were taken by myself, and unless otherwise stated were taken in March 2000.

Construction of Terminal One was completed in 1981 and the facility opened for operations on 1 July. More than half of Changi Airport's total land was reclaimed from the sea, and to make way for the construction of the airport which started in 1975, almost 200 hectares of swampland was cleared. This photograph shows the departure level – the arrivals level is situated below.

Terminal Two was completed and opened for operations on 22 November 1990 and is connected to Terminal One by a people-mover system (the Changi Skytrain). Landscaping at the airport is designed to achieve a tropical effect to soothe weary travellers, with tall majestic palm trees, colourful plants and ever-blooming flowers.

Singapore Changi is a wonderful airport to relax in. In the departure lounge of Terminal Two, departing and transit passengers may relax at The Orchid Garden set in a natural landscape of lush foliage around a carp pond.

Throughout the departure lounge are dotted well-stocked shops offering a wide selection of duty-free liquor, tobacco, perfumes and cosmetics, clothing, electronics and Singapore souvenirs. Stores are well planned and afford customers the chance to select purchases in a stress-free environment.

Passengers can take their pick of several eating and drinking establishments situated in the departure lounges. A wide variety of restaurants caters for all passengers' needs.

ABOVE AND OPPOSITE:
Terminal Two offers passengers 132 counters at which to check in for their flights. Moving around is stress-free in this large air-conditioned, modern and well designed facility.

As early evening approaches, the counters become busier as passengers arrive to check in for their overnight flights.

As part of Singapore's Millennium celebrations, two of the baggage carousels at the Terminal Two arrivals area were appropriately decorated and invited visitors to participate in the Millennia Mania celebrations. A stylised version of the figures '2000' is incorporated with a dragon in recognition that this was the Chinese year of the dragon. The most spectacular millennial celebrations in Asia took place in Singapore over a fifteen-month period from June 1999 until August 2000. Also portrayed here is the Merlion, the symbol of Singapore.

Thai Airways International has now replaced its fleet of Boeing 747 series 200 aircraft with the more modern series 300 and 400 machines, but when this photograph was taken in March 1989, the former type was a regular visitor to Singapore. Services to Changi Airport are now performed by Boeing's latest model – the Triple Seven – and Airbus A300s. In this picture of Boeing 747-200 HS-TGC, the push tractor is about to detach and the flight deck crew will then be given instructions to taxi to the departure runway.

ABOVE:
Air New Zealand Boeing 767 ZK-NBE is seen being prepared for a flight to Auckland at its gate on the west side of Terminal One in March 1989. At that time, ZK-NBE had been flying for the airline for a mere six months, and continued to do so for a further four years before entering service with the South American airline Transbrasil.

LEFT:
A Pelita Air Service Fokker 28 was photographed in April 1989 about to come to a halt after landing on runway 02L. This Indonesian carrier provided executive transportation plus general aviation services with a varied selection of aircraft and helicopters.

The background featured in this photograph of Malaysia Airlines Boeing 737 9M-MBK has altered dramatically since it was captured on film in April 1989. Other pages within this book illustrate the construction of additional gates and aircraft stands.

Photographed in April 1989 prior to the opening of Terminal Two, Garuda Indonesia Boeing 747 PK-GSC is seen slowly negotiating the taxiway soon after vacating its gate on the east side of Terminal One.

Pakistan International Airlines Airbus
Industrie A300 AP-BBA, photographed in
April 1989, catches the rays of the setting
sun as it is being prepared for departure at
its gate on the west side of Terminal One.
The carrier still provides a service on the
Karachi–Singapore route, a twice-weekly
flight operated today by one of the
company's A310 airliners.

LEFT:
Air Hong Kong commenced services in 1986 operating scheduled cargo flights. At the time the only aircraft in the fleet was a 707 and the classic Boeing airliner was photographed departing Singapore in April 1989. VR-HKK has commenced its take-off roll and has applied full power for take-off on runway 20L. This 707 continued to fly for Air Hong Kong until October 1992, and the airline now provides cargo services with a fleet of Boeing 747s.

BELOW:
Most of the grassed area seen in the background in this April 1989 photograph has since been converted to hard stands for parking aircraft. Malaysia Airlines Airbus Industrie A300 9M-MHB, carrying stickers inviting tourists to visit Malaysia, appears to be out of place in the present inclement conditions. However, such weather seldom lasts for long.

In 1989 Air Canada provided a regular service from Canada to Singapore, via Bombay. The aircraft operating the flight arrived at Changi in the morning and as the return service was not scheduled to depart until early evening, the aircraft was parked at a remote stand during the day. Boeing 747 C-GAGB was photographed in April 1989 whilst receiving the attention of the ground staff prior to being brought to a gate as the time for departure approached. The aircraft is fitted with a side cargo door, the rear section being configured to carry pallets of cargo.

The Dutch carrier Martinair put two Boeing 747s into service in 1987/8 which were configured to carry 530 economy class passengers or, after the removal of seating, freight loaded onto pallets via side cargo doors. PH-MCF was photographed in April 1991 about to depart the remote stand area.

In 1984 Singapore Airlines took delivery of four Boeing 757s which continued to provide service with the airline until early 1990. All four examples then found further service with American Trans Air following their withdrawal from the Singapore Airlines fleet. This photograph features 9V-SGN, which later became N752AT in the fleet of the American charter airline.

KLM's flights from Holland to destinations in the Far East were still performed by the carrier's fleet of Boeing 747 series 200 when PH-BUE was photographed in March 1989 as it departed its gate at Terminal One. The airliner had made an early morning arrival at Singapore following an overnight flight from Schiphol Airport and was about to leave on a service continuing to another Asian destination.

In summer 1983 Singapore Airlines took delivery of Boeing's latest jumbo at the time, the series 300 model. These aircraft entered service with the airline with the added inscription 'BIG TOP' placed on the upper fuselage. One of the American-registered airliners to receive the Singapore Airlines colours was N116KB, which also carried titles applied in italics instead of the regular lettering currently seen on the aircraft. The Boeing 747 was photographed in April 1990.

The Belgian airline SABENA currently uses Boeing 747s to fly its Brussels–Singapore service. In the early 1990s, five McDonnell Douglas DC-10s were included in the carrier's fleet and were regularly employed on the route, but this type no longer appears in the SABENA fleet having been replaced by two of the manu-facturer's subsequent model, the MD-11. When this photograph was taken in April 1990, the flight from Brussels had been performed by the fifth DC-10 to be delivered to SABENA, and OO-SLE was seen whilst being serviced in readiness for its next flight.

Boeing 737 series 200 9M-MBK is no longer a member of Malaysia's fleet having departed the airline in summer 1993. In this photograph, taken in April 1990, the airliner carried the company's previous livery and titles (the title 'Malaysian Airline System' has since been shortened to read 'Malaysia'). Note that at the time this, and other aircraft in the fleet, carried additional stickers promoting Malaysia as a tourist destination in 1990.

ABOVE AND LEFT:
Formed in 1975 and a member of the Singapore Airlines Group, Tradewinds changed its name in April 1992 and is now known as Silk Air. The airline currently operates scheduled passenger services from Singapore to surrounding destinations. McDonnell Douglas MD-87 9V-TRY entered service with the airline in January 1989 and continued to fly with the carrier until January 1991, alongside Boeing 737 series 300 aircraft which were put into service in Tradewinds colours in 1990. The latter type continued to fly for the company, later receiving Silk Air titles, until being replaced by Airbus Industrie A319 and A320 twin-jets. Boeing 737-300 9V-TRB was photographed in April 1991.

China Airlines provides a regular service between Taipei and Singapore, and currently uses Airbus Industrie A300s, the type having operated this service for a considerable time. A300 B-1800 was photographed at the terminal in April 1991 whilst receiving the attention of the ground crew prior to departure.

British Airways Boeing 747 series 400 G-BNLN was also photographed on the same day whilst parked at an adjacent stand. The aircraft was being re-stocked with food and refreshments during its short stop at Changi whilst *en route* to Australia.

Royal Brunei operated its first scheduled flight from the Brunei capital Bandar Seri Begawan to Singapore in 1975, a service which is still operated. In this April 1991 photograph, Boeing 757 V8-RBB, one of two of the type in service with the carrier, is being prepared for the return flight. In the background it can be seen that work on the construction of Terminal Two has commenced.

Boeing 767s have operated Scandinavian Airlines System's Copenhagen–Singapore services for more than ten years and the type still provides transportation on the route. When photographed in April 1991, LN-RCD had recently been delivered to the airline, and at the time of writing, still carries the SAS colours.

Royal Air Cambodge is the national airline
of Cambodia, operating international and
domestic services from Phnom Penh, the
country's capital city. A twice-weekly
service is operated between Phnom Penh
and Singapore, flights being performed by
the carrier's only Boeing 737 series 400,
9M-MMC, which was photographed upon
arrival at Changi in October 1998.

In October 1998 Silk Air was still operating services with its Boeing 737 series 300 aircraft, of which three examples carried the company colours. 9V-TRC was captured by the camera as the airliner was being pushed back from its gate at Terminal Two for an afternoon departure.

RIGHT:
Flights operated by various European airlines have arrived more or less at the same time. The aircraft are seen parked together alongside their Asian counterpart in this photograph taken in April 1990.

BELOW:
Saudi Arabian Airlines' weekly flight to Singapore is still flown by the carrier's Boeing 747-300s, a flight that stops off at Changi whilst flying from Jedda to Jakarta. HZ-AIS was operating this service when photographed in October 1998. It had just been pushed back from the gate and was awaiting instructions to taxi.

Garuda airliners make regular appearances at SIN and normally park at gates situated on Finger D. Boeing 737 series 500 PK-GGC was photographed in October 1998, whilst being pushed back for immediate departure.

In 1998 additional gates at the north end of
Finger D were constructed and this work
was well advanced in October when Air
India Airbus Industrie A310 VT-EJK was
photographed about to taxi past the site on
a return flight to the Indian sub-continent.

The extent of the construction work is clearly visible in this shot taken at the same time of China Airlines Airbus Industrie A300 B-196 taxying for departure after vacating its stand at one of the gates on Finger C. In the background, a Singapore Airlines Airbus A310 is about to land on runway 20L.

The Changi Skytrain connects Terminals One and Two and transports passengers over the 600-metre journey in one minute compared with a fifteen-minute walk. Trains are fully automated, quiet and efficient, and run at very frequent intervals throughout the day.

The airport emergency service is on the alert around the clock, with two strategically placed fully equipped fire stations capable of reaching the runway and being ready for action within three minutes. A third sub-fire station on the airport is ready to deal with fires in airport buildings.

Singapore Tower is an eighty-metre high
Air Traffic Control Centre with state-of-
the-art communication facilities and
navigational aids.

Singapore Airport in the Year 2000

Singapore Airlines Boeing 747 series 400 9V-SPL heads a line-up of airliners being prepared at gates in Terminal Two for early evening departures. Papa-Lima is due to depart for San Francisco at 17.00 hours, a one-stop flight of almost 8000 miles which will reach its destination at 17.30 hours local time on the same day.

Singapore Airlines is the national airline of Singapore, the island state linked by a causeway to the southernmost tip of the Malay Peninsula. Following the opening of Terminal Two in November 1990, all flights operated by the carrier originate from gates situated within this terminal, numbered E1–E12, E20–E28, F31–F42 and F50–F59. Boeing 747 series 400 9V-SMC sits proudly at gate E26 beneath the sign erected on top of the terminal buildings which welcomes travellers to Singapore. The airline is the main user of the terminal.

The driver of the tug has received instructions to push back Airbus Industrie A310 9V-STS from the gate. This aircraft is one of eighteen of the type used on the carrier's daily services.

When an airliner arrives after a long-haul flight it is surrounded by ground equipment and staff who prepare the aircraft for its next flight. Here we witness the loading of bags in the rear compartment and containers in the forward compartment of Boeing 747 series 400 9V-SMH in preparation for its next long distance flight.

LEFT AND BELOW:
Singapore Airlines has its own dedicated engineering company and within its hangars the company's aircraft receive regular servicing and attention. In these two photographs, several members of the company fleet are seen receiving the attention of the engineers.

RIGHT AND BELOW:
The departure of Singapore Airlines flight SQ2 to San Francisco, operated by Boeing 747-400 9V-SPL sporting the tropical 'Megatop' colours, appears to have brought on a tropical storm. Two 747s operated in this colour scheme, which was applied to introduce the revamping and upgrading of the carrier's First, Raffles and Economy Class services.

Following the departure of the jumbo in the tropical colour scheme, one of Singapore Airlines' recently delivered Boeing 777s taxied and turned onto runway 20L. 9V-SRD is one of ten of the first batch of the series 200 type flown by the airline and bears the title 'Jubilee'.

Making a touchdown before a downpour is
Boeing 747 series 400 9V-SMA, the first
'Megatop' to be delivered to Singapore
Airlines in March 1989.

Boeing 747 series 400 9V-SPJ is seen about to put all its wheels onto the tarmac of runway 02R in the early morning. The large building in the background provides the in-flight meals for Singapore Airlines.

Singapore Airlines also operates its long-haul services with a fleet of Airbus Industrie A340 airliners. 9V-SJL is a series 300 model, of which the carrier currently has seventeen examples in service. At the time of writing five series 500 models were on order.

The Airbus A340s in the Singapore Airlines fleet are also identified by class name, and the title 'Celestar' has been applied to their upper fuselages. 9V-SJG has been flying for the airline since being delivered fresh from the Airbus plant in March 1997, and is here seen about to land on runway 02L.

Shortly after the arrival of Airbus A340
9V-SJG, another of this manufacturer's
products adorned with the Singapore
Airlines colours was seen on approach to
runway 02L. Airbus A310 9V-STZ was the
last of the type to join the airline and has
served the carrier since autumn 1992.

Singapore Airlines operates eight dedicated freighters, all being Boeing 747 series 400s and bearing the 'Mega Ark' inscription on the upper fuselage. Whilst the passenger-carrying version of the series 400 aircraft has an extended upper deck, the specially constructed cargo-carrying version does not. 9V-SFB is about to commence its take-off roll on runway 02L.

RIGHT:
Boeing 737 series 800 B-18610 was the latest aircraft to be delivered to China Airlines when photographed proceeding to a gate on Finger D. The airliner entered service with China Airlines in December 1999 and when outstanding orders for the type are fulfilled, a total of fifteen will carry the airline's colours.

BELOW:
Bouraq offers services to and from the Indonesian city Surabaya. The airline's Boeing 737 series 200 aircraft provide a daily flight which arrives and departs Singapore at midday. PK-IJK is seen at its gate being prepared and refuelled prior to departing on its return flight of 856 miles.

Garuda is another Indonesian airline that flies to Changi. Several daily flights flown by the carrier's Boeing 737 series 300 airliners provide services between Singapore and Jakarta. PK-GGO is seen upon arrival operating the morning flight from the Indonesian capital.

The midday arrivals at three 'D' gates receive the attention of the ground crews whilst awaiting departure to their various destinations.

China Airlines Boeing 737-800 B-18610 arrived at its gate earlier, and has now been joined by Airbus Industrie A300 B-18551, which has occupied the adjacent gate following a non-stop flight from Taipei.

ABOVE AND RIGHT:
A twice-weekly service from the Nepalese capital Kathmandu is currently scheduled to arrive at Singapore in the late afternoon following its one-stop flight of over 2000 miles. This service is performed by one of two Boeing 757s in the Royal Nepal Airlines fleet. On this occasion 9N-ACA was operating the service and was photographed approaching its allocated gate on Finger C. The airline's titles appear in Nepali on the starboard side, and in English on the port side.

Japan Airlines uses the facilities provided by Terminal One. McDonnell Douglas MD-11 JA8585 is being prepared for a flight prior to the boarding of its passengers. The crew of SATS (Singapore Airport Terminal Services) will ensure that all the requirements necessary for a comfortable flight are fulfilled.

The aircraft operating the daily flight from Surabaya provided by the Indonesian airline Bouraq was again photographed as it approached its gate on Finger D. Although the carrier has four Boeing 737s in its fleet, PK-IJK is again the aircraft being used on this service.

Up to two services a week from Singapore to the Bangladesh capital Dhaka are provided by Biman Bangladesh, flights being operated by both McDonnell Douglas DC-10s and Airbus Industrie A310s. On this occasion the service was being performed by S2-ADF, one of two A310s in the company fleet. It was photographed during the push-back operation from its gate at Terminal One.

One of Royal Brunei's services is a flight from London–Heathrow to Bandar Seri Begawan, which stops at Dubai and Singapore prior to reaching its final destination. Following its flight from Dubai, the aircraft remains on the ground in Singapore for about one hour before commencing the final leg of its journey. In this photograph Boeing 767 V8-RBG is again airborne for the remaining 800 miles of a 7000-mile journey from London.

Thai Airways International aircraft are regular visitors to Singapore and the carrier's newly delivered series 300 Boeing 777s provide transportation for passengers flying from Bangkok. This latest Boeing aircraft has the capacity for more than 300 passengers. The early morning flight from Bangkok is being operated this time by HS-TKD, which is turning to line up with the gate at Terminal One.

As well as transporting passengers, the holds of the Triple Sevens are configured to accept pallet-loads of cargo which are loaded on and off at the gate area whilst passengers disembark. The pallets carried on this particular flight are covered by what could be termed 'colour co-ordinated' plastic sheeting.

The arrival of the Thai Airways International Triple Seven has attracted the attention of local retirees who congregate on a daily basis in the air-conditioned comfort of the terminal building, and can be heard vociferously discussing the world's problems.

Tango-Kilo-Delta has completed its turnround operation and, after leaving the gate, slowly proceeds to runway 02L for departure, overtaken by Eva Air Cargo McDonnell Douglas MD-11 B-16107 which had earlier vacated its stand at the west cargo area.

Myanmar Airways International was formed by the Myanmar Government-owned Myanmar Airways to operate scheduled international passenger services from Yangon. These services now operate to Bangkok, Hong Kong, Kuala Lumpur and Singapore. The carrier's Boeing 737 series 400 9M-MMH flies to Singapore twice a week and is seen negotiating the central apron area prior to coming to a halt at its gate on Finger C.

Australia's airline QANTAS is a regular visitor to Terminal One and shares flights to Australia with other major carriers using Singapore Airport. The route is extremely popular and several cities in Australia are served, with flights transporting holiday-makers and business people who both visit Singapore and transit through the airport whilst *en route* to other Far Eastern destinations. Boeing 767 VH-OGN is about to return to its homeland and will no doubt be back within a few days.

Boeing's newest wide-body, the 777, has attracted the attention of many of the world's airlines and several, including Emirates, have put the aircraft into service. Emirates' daily flight from Dubai to Melbourne, Australia, is operated by the type and stops off in Singapore prior to completing the second sector of its journey. A6-EMJ is seen upon arrival at its gate on the west side of Changi Airport. It carries an advertisement promoting the annual shopping festival held in Dubai each March.

Air Madagascar's flight from Antananarivo to Singapore arrives around 06.00 hours and does not return until the early hours of the following day. In order to avoid occupying a gate that can be used by other carriers, the aircraft is towed to a remote stand where it will remain until being brought back to a gate to board passengers for its return flight to Madagascar. Boeing 747 series 200 5R-MFT, photographed whilst parked at the north apron, was delivered new to the carrier in January 1979 and is a combi-model, configured to carry pallets as well as passengers.

A comprehensive service is operated
between Singapore and Hong Kong, and
Cathay Pacific utilises a variety of aircraft
on its flights. A late afternoon service was
being operated by B-HOP, one of the
carrier's Boeing 747-400s, when it was
photographed about to apply full power for
take-off on runway 20L at the start of a
flight to Hong Kong.

Thai Airways International has examples of the Boeing 777 in its extensive fleet, and the carrier has selected the series 200 model. Members of the fleet are regular visitors to Changi, and one of these airliners, HS-TJD, is seen at the airport bearing additional stickers applied to commemorate the seventy-second birthday of the King of Thailand. The airliner is about to depart from runway 02R, whilst in the distance the aircraft operating the British Airways overnight flight from London-Heathrow is about to touch down on runway 02L.

Following the departure of the Thai Boeing 777, Cathay Pacific Airbus Industrie A330 B-HLE taxied to the same runway and positioned for take-off. This airline has twelve examples of the type, which are configured to carry 314 passengers in a two-class layout.

Singapore Tower and Terminal Two can be seen in this photograph of two Singapore Airlines Boeing 747 series 400 'Megatops' at their gates whilst being prepared for flight. They were photographed from the eastern perimeter.

Singapore's other passenger-carrying airline, Silk Air, which is 100% owned by Singapore Airlines, introduced the Airbus Industrie A320 to its fleet in the latter part of 1998, and the type operates on scheduled services to destinations within the region. Airbus Industrie A320 9V-SLA was the first of the type to receive the Silk Air livery and is seen about to make an early morning departure.

Seen here operating a morning service into the airport is one of Malaysia Airlines' extended-range series 200 Boeing 777s. 9M-MRB is seen gently touching down onto runway 02R.

The Airbus Industrie A300 airliner has featured in the Thai Airways International fleet since the airline put its first example into service in 1979. Deliveries of different variants of the type have continued throughout the following twenty years, and the airline now counts twenty-five examples in its fleet. In this photograph one of the more recent aircraft to be delivered, HS-TAT, is about to take off on runway 02R.

Runway 02R is also being used for the departure of Philippine Airlines' morning flight to Manila, operated by Airbus Industrie A330 F-OHZS. The fact that the aircraft is leased from Airbus Industrie Financial Services accounts for the French registration.

Aircraft carrying the colours of Hong Kong-based Cathay Pacific are regular visitors to Singapore and all aircraft types flown by the carrier can be observed at SIN at one time or another. Airbus Industrie A330 B-HLF has flown over the airport perimeter fence and is about to touch down on runway 02R.

Cargo plays a very important part in Changi Airport's operations and airliners configured purely for the transportation of freight appear with great regularity. Whilst the largest percentage of this traffic occurs during the hours of darkness, it is still possible to observe a proportion during daylight hours. The American international cargo airline Polar Air Cargo includes Asia in its routes and one of the carrier's Boeing 747s, N850FT, was photographed at the east cargo area prior to departure.

The Minebea Group of Companies manufactures airline-related materials and was represented at a recent Asian Aerospace exhibition held in Singapore. This McDonnell Douglas DC-10, N10MB, is the company corporate jet.

Angel Air is one of Thailand's newest carriers and was formed in 1998, operating from Bangkok International Airport. The airline provides scheduled services to a number of regional destinations including daily flights between Bangkok and Singapore. The first flight of the day, the 07.50 hours service to Bangkok, has just been pushed back from the gate and Boeing 737 series 400 9M-MME is about to commence its 900-mile journey to Thailand.

Cathay Pacific's first flight of the day to Hong Kong, CX710 departing Singapore at 08.05 hours, is not necessarily operated by the same type of aircraft each day. According to the OAG flight guide, several types are programmed to operate this service. On the day of this photograph however, Airbus Industrie A340 B-HXJ was provided, and is seen departing the ramp area for take-off on runway 02L.

A daily morning service to Beijing is provided by Air China and this flight delivers its passengers to the Chinese capital in the late afternoon. Boeing 767s operate these flights which depart SIN around 09.40 hours. On this occasion B-2552, one of six extended-range models in the Air China fleet, was operating the service. It is here seen negotiating the ramp area, safely passing other airliners at their gates.

Indian Airlines, India's largest airline, shares Singapore services with the country's other major carrier Air India. A daily service from Chennai links the southern part of India with Singapore, flights being operated by one of Indian Airlines' Airbus Industrie A300s. VT-EHD is seen departing for Chennai. The building behind the aircraft is the main fire department serving the airport.

Passengers bound for Tokyo from Singapore have a choice of carriers, with four airlines currently operating on the route. One of the morning flights is provided by Japan Airlines. It departs Singapore at 08.35 hours, and following a non-stop flight of 3300 miles, its passengers reach the Japanese capital by 16.00 hours local time. The airliner providing transportation for this flight when photographed was McDonnell Douglas MD-11 JA8580, one of the carrier's 'J Birds'. This particular aircraft bears the illustration of a tufted puffin.

Singapore is one of China Airlines' scheduled destinations for cargo flights, with regular flights operating from Taipei. On this occasion Boeing 747 series 200 B-18751 had been observed earlier in the morning being unloaded and loaded at the east cargo area, prior to taxying the full length of the 20L/02R taxiway where it is seen turning for take-off.

Air India's service from Mumbai has just arrived and the aircraft is seen taxying within the central apron whilst slowly approaching its gate. Airbus Industrie A310 VT-EJK was the aircraft assigned to the service, and it is interesting to note that the same aircraft was photographed operating this flight in October 1998 (see page 38).

Another aircraft to be towed away from a gate until the time approaches for departure is Airbus Industrie A340 3B-NBD of Air Mauritius. The carrier flies to Singapore twice a week, and the airliner will remain at its remote stand until late afternoon, when it will be moved to a gate to be prepared for an early evening flight to the island situated in the Indian Ocean.

Vietnam Airlines Airbus Industrie A320
S7-ASE has just lifted off runway 02L to
start its journey to Ho Chi Minh and Hanoi.

British Airways Boeing 747 series 400 G-BYGF arrived from London around ninety minutes earlier and Speedbird 011 is now about to depart on the second part of its journey to Perth, Australia. The Thai Airways International Airbus A300 taxying to the runway will take off in front of the BA airliner which is still stationary.

RIGHT AND BELOW:
The ground staff have completed their tasks and Golf-Foxtrot has been given instructions from the tower to taxi. Upon departure, the jumbo will have a further 2400 miles to fly before reaching its final destination, over 9000 miles from London.

China Southern Boeing 777 B-2058 is seen at its gate being prepared for departure to mainland China. A daily service to Guang-zhou, then on to Beijing and Xiamen on certain days, is offered by the carrier.

Eva Air is a major Taiwanese airline and operates a daily service to Singapore from its base in Taipei, a non-stop flight of 2000 miles scheduled to be operated by a Boeing 747 series 400. N409EV has just arrived and is about to come to a halt at its gate. N409EV is configured for only 110 passengers in three classes, the remaining available space being set aside for pallets.

One of the carriers using Terminal Two is Malaysia Airlines, the majority of the carrier's flights operating on the short Singapore to Kuala Lumpur route. Two of Malaysia Airlines' aircraft are seen being prepared for departure in this photograph showing Boeing 737 series 400 9M-MMT in the foreground, and Boeing 737 series 500 9M-MFC at an adjacent gate.

Air France operates a daily service connecting Paris with Singapore, a flight timed to arrive in the early afternoon. This non-stop service is operated by the carrier's Boeing 777s. On this occasion F-GSPH was operating the day's flight.

Saudi Arabian Airlines' service from Jedda to Singapore is operated twice-weekly with Boeing 747 series 300s. Making a visit to Changi on this occasion however was one of the airline's McDonnell Douglas MD-11 airliners which carries the special registration HZ-HM8, signifying that the aircraft is a member of the Saudi Arabian VIP fleet. This concern is a division of Saudi Arabian Airlines and operates non-commercial VIP flights.

Mid-afternoon sees the commencement of a batch of arriving traffic, one of the first to arrive being a Cathay Pacific service operated by Boeing 747 series 400 B-HOV, here seen about to land on runway 02L.

Following closely behind the Cathay jumbo was Turkish Airlines Airbus Industrie A340 TC-JDJ, bringing its passengers from Istanbul. The airliner will remain on the ground for seven hours before returning to Turkey, an overnight service routed via Bangkok.

Boeing 747 PH-BUH of the Dutch airline KLM was photographed upon arrival at the east cargo ramp. This aircraft is one of two dedicated freighters in the KLM fleet, and it will be observed that unlike other regular series 200 models, this aircraft has been modified and given the stretched upper deck normally associated with the manufacturer's series 300 and 400 types.

Long-haul arrivals are interspersed with domestic and freight traffic, one of the domestic arrivals to appear being Silk Air Airbus Industrie A319 9V-SBB, which was photographed landing on runway 02L following a flight from the Thai tourist resort Chiang Mai. Services to this destination are provided exclusively by Silk Air.

Bangkok Airways is a long established airline and has served the region since its formation in 1968. Its small fleet is made up entirely of ATR 72 propeller-driven aircraft configured for seventy passengers. The daily service linking Koh Samui, one of Thailand's island resorts, with Singapore, is being operated by HS-PGH, which is within a few metres of landing at Changi following its non-stop flight. Upon the runway being vacated, the Singapore Airlines freighter seen to the left of the picture will taxi and hold on the runway until given instructions to apply power for take-off.

One of the major cargo carriers to serve Singapore is the North American airline FedEx and its aircraft are to be seen at the airport on most, if not all, days. After coming to a halt on the runway, McDonnell Douglas MD-11 N619FE will taxi to the east cargo area for unloading.

Eva Air also uses McDonnell Douglas MD-11 cargo-configured aircraft and has nine of the type operating its freight services to seventeen international destinations. Singapore is one of this Taiwanese airline's destinations and B-16109 was photographed as it turned onto the runway for take-off.

Thai Airways International Airbus Industrie A300 HS-TAM has just about completed its non-stop journey from Bangkok and is a few seconds from touchdown. This airline is one of the major carriers on the route with several flights a day.

The staff in the control tower have an uninterrupted view of arrivals and departures and have witnessed the safe arrival of Emirates Boeing 777 A6-EME, which has gently placed its landing gear onto the runway following a flight from Dubai.

Sri Lanka's national airline, now known as SriLankan Airlines, operates a thrice-weekly flight between Colombo and Singapore, a service that continues to Kuala Lumpur. Airbus Industrie A340 4R-ADB had previously arrived from the Malaysian capital, and following the boarding of its Singapore passengers, taxied for take-off on its final sector of a flight back to Colombo. Alpha-Delta-Bravo had yet to receive the company's new title and colours and is seen with the airline's old name 'AirLanka' and the colours associated with that name.

SriLankan Airlines currently has four Airbus A340 airliners in its fleet. 4R-ADA, the first example to be delivered to the carrier in autumn 1994, has been given the new company titles and colours.

One of the European services is a daily flight from the Swiss city Zurich, operated by McDonnell Douglas MD-11s of the Swissair fleet. HB-IWO was photographed at the end of its journey. After landing it will taxi to a gate in Terminal Two.

The majority of long-haul traffic passing through Changi does so after dark; in fact Changi is another airport that never sleeps. Air New Zealand's lunchtime flight is one of the first evening arrivals into SIN which, after receiving servicing and boarding passengers, leaves its Terminal Two gate for an overnight return to Christchurch. Boeing 767 ZK-NCK is awaiting the containers holding passengers' luggage which will be loaded into the rear compartments of the aircraft.